The Efficient, Inventive (Often Annoying)

MELVIL DEWEY

400-499 PHILOLOGY
300-399 SOCIOLOGY
200-299 THEOLOGY
100-199 PHILOSOPHY
000-099 GENERAL WORKS

500-599 NATURAL SCIENCE
600-699 USEFUL ARTS
700-799 FINE ARTS
800-899 LITERATURE
900-999 HISTORY

Alexis O'Neill

Illustrated by Edwin Fotheringham

CALKINS CREEK
AN IMPRINT OF BOYDS MILLS & KANE
New York

"My heart is open to anything that's either decimal or about libraries."
—Melvil Dewey

Melvil Dewey loves putting things in order.

Oh, no—what's he doing now?

He's organizing the chaos of his mother's kitchen cupboard. And now the cellar.

There. Nice and neat.

Melvil loves keeping track of things.

He's recording his height. His weight. How much money he has earned.

Melvil loves books. He tucks his money into his pocket and goes for a ten-mile walk.

Wait—where is he going?

— *Melvil*

— Melville

— Melville

— Melville

Melvil treks ten miles from his home in Adams Center, New York, to Watertown. He buys an unabridged *Webster's American Dictionary of the English Language*—the biggest, thickest book in the shop. And inside that book? Words in tidy lists! Words in alphabetical order! Easy-to-find, delicious words! Then he rushes back home.

WATERTOWN-10

After locking his father's shop at night, Melvil sometimes stretches out on the leather hides in the storeroom. He wonders, *What will I do with my life?*

He wants to leave the world better than he found it. But he doesn't know quite how. Not yet.

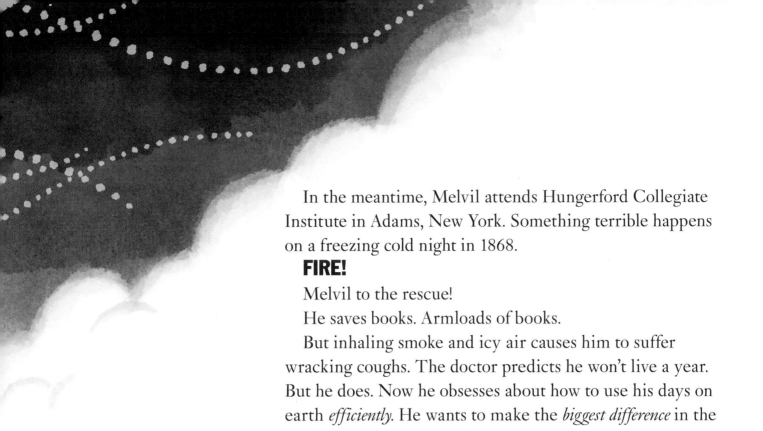

In the meantime, Melvil attends Hungerford Collegiate Institute in Adams, New York. Something terrible happens on a freezing cold night in 1868.

FIRE!

Melvil to the rescue!

He saves books. Armloads of books.

But inhaling smoke and icy air causes him to suffer wracking coughs. The doctor predicts he won't live a year. But he does. Now he obsesses about how to use his days on earth *efficiently.* He wants to make the *biggest difference* in the world *in the least amount of time.*

Melvil notices that lots of new immigrants are flooding into America. Many of them can't read English yet. They need an education—fast, fast, **FAST!**

Hold on—
THAT'S IT!

He will help people get their hands on good books. After all, "reading is a mighty engine, beside which steam and electricity sink into insignificance," he writes. Books will give them a good education. *Efficiently.* **THAT** will make a big difference in the world!

But first Melvil needs to get an education himself. At Amherst College, he studies. He's at the college library. All. The. Time. He even gets a job there. But hardly anyone ever uses it. Melvil can't blame them. How **INEFFICIENT!**

Amherst's thirty thousand books are arranged by shelf number, not subject. When there are too many books for a shelf, the whole collection has to be rearranged. Look at all the **TIME** it takes to find the book you want.

Before long, Melvil takes care of **THAT** problem.

Ah! How he loves books and libraries! But usually, only rich people and expensive schools have them. How can you read if you don't have money to buy books or pay for college?

Melvil has a brainstorm.

Why not provide the **BEST** reading for the **LARGEST** number of people at the **LEAST** cost! Why not promote **FREE PUBLIC LIBRARIES** for everyone! People can **BORROW** books instead of **BUYING** them or **PAYING** to subscribe to a service. (This is not a new idea, but no one is as **NOISY** and **PERSISTENT** as Melvil about pushing for it for everyone.)

But do you know what a **BIG PROBLEM** is?

No two libraries shelve books the same way. Some do it by the author's last name. Some do it by the size of the book. Some do it by the color of the cover. Some even stack books from floor to ceiling.

WHAT A HODGE-PODGE.

Night and day, Melvil dreams about ways to organize libraries. He dreams about numbers and decimals. He is in **LOVE** with decimals and libraries.

One Sunday during chapel at Amherst . . .

EUREKA!

He gets the idea of using **NUMBERS** *and* **DECIMALS** to organize library books.

With a consistent numbering system, it would be easy to find exactly where a book was located, no matter which library you were visiting.

Melvil is fired up.

He visits libraries all over the Northeast. He reads other people's ideas about organizing collections. Then he invents his own classification system.

Melvil assigns numbers to ten broad classes of knowledge. (History = 900s! Science = 500s! Arts = 700s!) Then he divides classes into ten divisions and each division into ten sections with decimals to show specific subclasses. Numbers are written on spines of books. Books sit neatly in order on shelves. Totally **EFFICIENT!**

The trustees at Columbia College in New York are impressed. They invite him to become their chief librarian. But they don't know what a zealot they have brought to their campus.

Melvil thinks big. In addition to working in the library, he wants to open a school at Columbia to train librarians. Librarians would educate readers and guide them to the highest-quality books through "best books" lists. He thinks college-educated women would be **TERRIFIC** in this profession. They have clear heads, strong hands, and great hearts. (Also, they will work for less money than men.)

Columbia College SCHOOL OF LIBRARY ECONOMY

No problem, right?

Wrong.

Columbia trustees do **NOT** want women on their campus. Period. Only men. Do you understand this, Melvil?

But Melvil ignores their roars. He figures once they see his school in action, they'll *purrrrr*!

He advertises for students. Twenty sign up. Seventeen of them are women.

He sets up a library school in a storeroom above the chapel across the street from the Columbia campus. (Technically, it's not a classroom, he figures, so technically he's not breaking any rules . . .)

The students think Melvil is energetic! Awesome!

. . . and odd.

Melvil rushes into the classroom at the last minute, delivers a lecture at 180 words per minute, then rushes out.

He invents ways to keep libraries **QUIET** so patrons can read and study. Rubber tips on chairs and tables. Rubber wheels on book trucks. Slippers for library workers. He tells people to whisper at the loan desk and **NO TALKING AT ALL** everywhere else.

He invents ways to be efficient. A pencil with one end blue, the other red. A ruler narrow at the low numbers, wider at the higher numbers. A hanging vertical file.

And Melvil always writes in shorthand or in simplified spelling on recycled library catalog cards—*tho, altho, thoro, thru, jumpt, soundz . . .* Why, he's even gotten rid of silent letters in his name so that **MELVILLE** has become **MELVIL**.

Melvil is a whirlwind! He pushes, pushes, **PUSHES** his ideas on people. His brain can hardly keep up with all the ideas he has. He wants to see changes **RIGHT AWAY**. This makes people angry. They tell him to **SIT STILL** and **BE QUIET**. *Shhh!*

But do you think Melvil sits still?

NO!

He wants to do more and more and **MORE**.

He becomes State Librarian and Secretary to the Board of Regents of the University of the State of New York. He organizes the New York State Library Association. He provides books for the blind. He launches a traveling library system. He helps form the Children's Library Association. (Whew!)

Boy! Some people **LOVE** Melvil: Efficient! Hardworking! Determined! Visionary!

Other people do **NOT** love Melvil: Controlling! Demanding! Manipulative! Glib-tongued!

But whether people find him appealing or annoying, the one thing that they agree on is that . . .

. . . Melvil Dewey **DID** make a difference in the world. He organized library collections, educated librarians, and championed free libraries for everyone.

A pretty good legacy for a boy who organized his mother's cupboard and walked ten miles to buy a dictionary, don't you think?

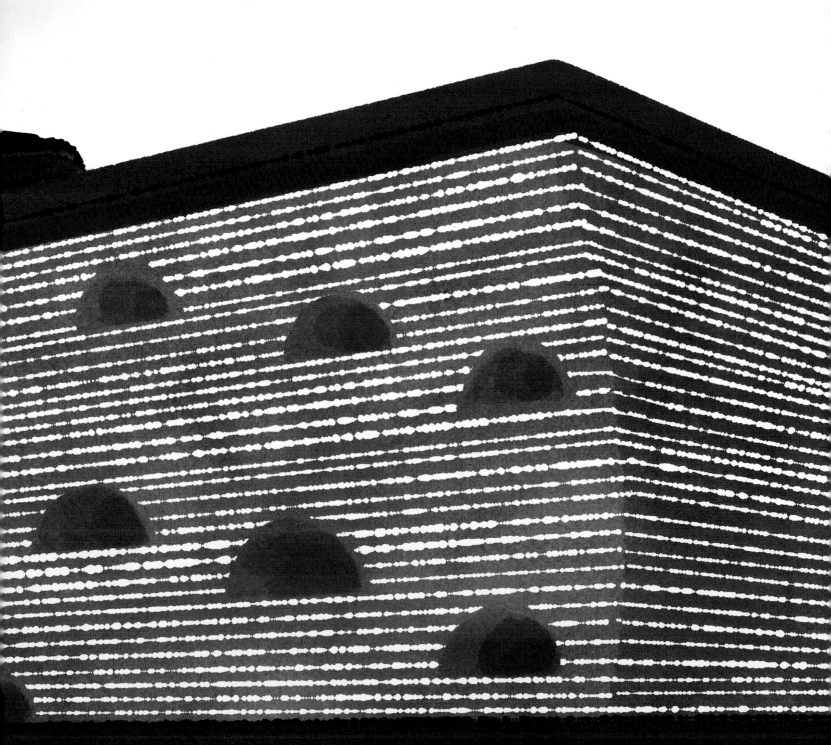

Melvil Dewey

Author's Note

Melvil Dewey ate, drank, slept, and talked libraries and library work. But Dewey had an enormous ego, a penchant for constantly challenging authority with his actions, and a knack for inflaming colleagues with his words. His behavior could be odd, annoying, and often unacceptable. In his later life, his harassment of women ultimately led to his being forced out of the American Library Association (ALA), an organization he helped form, and posthumously having his name stripped from its highest honor. In addition, his antisemitism and racism, evident in his exclusion of Jews and people of other religious and ethnic groups from his social and recreational resort, the Lake Placid Club, cost him his position as New York State Librarian. And yet, throughout his life and beyond, he had a tremendous influence on the many institutions and practices he created and shaped. In spite of his personal shortcomings, Dewey's accomplishments live on three major ways:

- in the way information is stored and retrieved in libraries today
- in the "best books" lists that are continually generated by all types of libraries for their users
- in the formal library schools that have trained countless librarians through the years who in turn have taught library users how to find items for themselves efficiently.

By the time of his death in 1931, the Dewey Decimal Classification (DDC) system was being used in over 96 percent of all American libraries. Today, libraries in more than 135 countries use the system to organize their collections for their users.

Timeline

1851	Melville Louis Kossuth Dewey is born on December 10, Adams Center, New York.
1864	Pays $10 for a copy of *Webster's Dictionary*.
1868	Attends Hungerford Collegiate Institute.
1869	Decides that higher education for the masses will be his lifelong cause.
1870	Becomes one of seventy-four members of the Amherst College class of 1874.
1873	Creates preliminary draft of the Dewey Decimal Classification system.
1874	Begins organizing Amherst College's library collection. Drops the "le" from Melville.
1875	Hired as assistant librarian at Amherst College. Completes forty-two-page *A Classification and Subject Index for Cataloguing and Arranging Books and Pamphlets of a Library*.
1876	Copyrights the Dewey Decimal Classification system.
1876	Helps start the American Library Association.
1878	Marries Annie Godfrey, Wellesley College's first librarian.
1883–1888	Serves as chief librarian of Columbia College (now University).
1885	Helps form the Children's Library Association.
1885	Publishes the second edition of the decimal classification scheme.
1887	Opens the first School of Library Economy at Columbia College. Son Godfrey is born.
1888–1919	Andrew Carnegie pays to build 1,689 public libraries in the U.S.
1889	Named State Librarian and Secretary to the Board of Regents of the University of the State of New York. Transfers the School of Library Economy from Columbia College to Albany, NY.
1890	Organizes the New York State Library Association. Elected president of the American Library Association.
1892	Re-elected president of the American Library Association.
1895	Establishes the Lake Placid Club, a community that excludes Jews and people of other religious and ethnic groups.
1899	Resigns from his position as Secretary to the Board of Regents of the University of the State of New York.
1905	Censured by the Board of Regents for conducting a private business, with discriminatory practices, while serving in a public position.
1906	Under pressure from Board of Regents, resigns from his positions as State Librarian and director of the library school.
1912	Becomes a management consultant focused on organizing organizations.
1922	Wife, Annie Godfrey, dies on August 25.
1924	Marries Emily Beal on May 28.
1931	Melvil Dewey dies on December 26, Lake Placid, Florida.

Dewey's Other Reform Passions

In addition to libraries, Dewey had other passions for reform, all centering on simplicity and efficiency:

Use of shorthand: He used a phonetic shorthand technique, Lindsley's Tachygraphy, to make efficient use of time as he wrote diary entries, letters, and notes to himself. He believed others should, too.

Metric reform: He disliked the "complicated" system of weights and measures (inches, feet, pounds, ounces) used in the United States. He proposed a shift to the metric system, in which units of measure are in multiples of ten.

Spelling reform: He thought that everyone could learn the English language more quickly if spellings were simplified. For example, he changed the spelling of his name from "Melville" to "Melvil." He tried to change "Dewey" to "Dui," but many thought it was just too eccentric. Here are other examples of simplified spellings:

"-ed" at the end of a word became "-t" (jumped to jumpt)

Silent letters were removed (Melville to Melvil)

"-re" endings were changed to "-er" (theatre to theater)

"ough" was changed to "o" when the "o" was long (though to tho)

"s" became a "z" when the "s" sounded like a "z" (sounds to soundz)

While spelling reform never took hold officially, we see evidence of it today in the abbreviated spellings used in casual email and text messages:

you to U

when to wen

are to R

to, too to 2

Simplified spellings have caught on in popular culture, just not in the way Dewey envisioned.

"To my thinking, a great librarian must have a clear head, a strong hand, and, above all, a great heart . . . and when I look into the future, I am inclined to think that most of the men who achieve this greatness will be women."

Melvil Dewey (top row, center) and the second library school class at New York City's Columbia College

"A library's function is to give the public in the quickest and cheapest way: information, inspiration, and recreation. If a better way than the book can be found, we should use it."

Dewey Decimal Classification System (DDC)

The Dewey Decimal Classification system is divided into **ten main classes** that cover the entire world of knowledge (each represented by the first digit). Each class is divided into **ten divisions** (the second digit). Each division has **ten sections** (the third digit). A decimal point follows the third digit in a class number, after which division by ten continues to the specific degree of classification needed.

Question: Are there elephants in the library?

Answer: Yes!

Science = **5**00 (First number = main class of world knowledge)

Animals = **59**0 (Second number = a subdivision of knowledge)

Mammals = **599** (Third number = a subsection of a subdivision of knowledge)

*Elephants = 599.***6***!* (Decimal = a specific degree of classification of the subsection of a subdivision of knowledge)

"Reading is a mighty engine, beside which steam and electricity sink into insignificance."

Selected Sources*

All quotations in the book can be found in the following sources marked with a double asterisk (**).

Battles, Matthew. *Library: An Unquiet History.* New York: W. W. Norton, 2015.

Dawe, George Grosvenor. *Melvil Dewey: Seer, Inspirer, Doer, 1851–1931.* New York: Lake Placid Club, 1932.

"Dewey Decimal Classification Summaries: A Brief Introduction to the Dewey Decimal Classification." oclc.org/en/dewey/features/summaries.html.

Dewey, Melvil. *Decimal Classification and Relativ Index for Arranging, Cataloging, and Indexing Rerums,* etc. Second Edition, Revised and Greatly Enlarged. Boston: Library Bureau, 1885.

Kendall, Joshua. "Information Technology: Melvil Dewey—The Librarian Who Worshipped Perfect Tens." In *America's Obsessives: The Compulsive Energy That Built a Nation,* pp. 86–117. New York: Grand Central Publishing, 2013.

**Koehler, Wallace. *Ethics and Values in Librarianship: A History.* Lanham, MD: Rowman & Littlefield Publishers, 2015.

Murray, Stuart A. P. *The Library: An Illustrated History.* Chicago: Skyhorse Publishing/American Library Association, 2009.

Rider, Fremont. *Melvil Dewey.* Chicago: American Library Association, 1944.

**Wiegand, Wayne A. *Irrepressible Reformer: A Biography of Melvil Dewey.* Chicago: American Library.

*websites active at time of publication

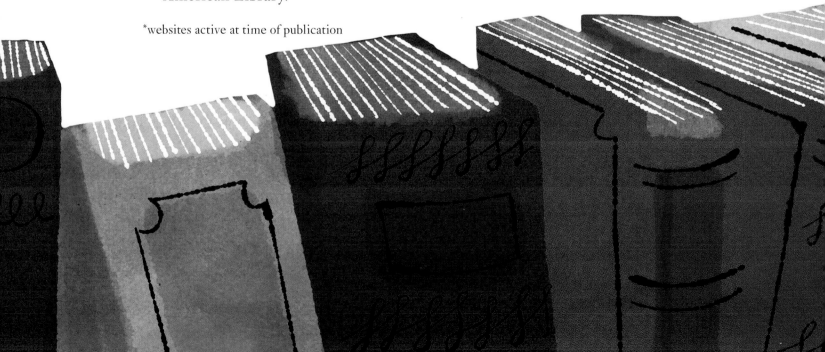

To librarians everywhere and all the good they bring to the world.
—AO

For my family
—EF

Acknowledgments

Thanks to Wayne A. Wiegand, who inspired me by making Melvil Dewey 3-D in his outstanding biography; to librarian friends, René, Holly, and Angelica, who told me to go for it; and to my writing friends who encouraged me through each draft.

Picture credits

Rare Book and Manuscript Library, Columbia University in the City of New York: 34, 37

For information about permission to reproduce selections from this book, please contact permissions@bmkbooks.com.

Calkins Creek
An imprint of Boyds Mills & Kane,
a division of Astra Publishing House
calkinscreekbooks.com
Printed in China

ISBN: 978-1-68437-198-3
Library of Congress Control Number: 2019954195

First edition
10 9 8 7 6 5 4 3 2 1

The text is set in Janson MT.
The titles are set in Franklin Gothic Condensed.
The illustrations are digital.